CATCH

Robert Smith and The Cure

DANIEL PATTON

GW00502512

THE DUNCE DIRECTIVE

PASSION

faith

MADNESS

23

DESIRE

(32)

If you were stranded on a desert island and you could only have one book, one record and one canned food item, what would they be?

The Encyclopaedia Britannica. Beethoven's nine symphonies. Mandarin oranges.

What is your favourite brand and shade of lipstick?

Jane's cosmetics 'reddest'

If there was an opportunity for you to jump into an alternate lifestyle, what would it be? **Astronaut**

What five words best describe you?

Inquisitive

Thoughtful

Stupid

Wishful

Alien

What would you do if a die-hard fan ran up to you in a pink jock strap on stage during a concert in order to prove his or her love for you?

I'd rather have flowers

Q&A © 1997 Canoe Limited Partnership

PASSION

*It's not a case of doing what's right, it's just the way I feel
that matters.*
Play For Today

Robert Smith is now a bona fide celebrity. In *Debrett* — the who's
who of high society — he lists his hobbies as "deep sea diving, hot
air ballooning, reading, writing and staring into space." Yet another
bizarre accolade for a man who once wore a bear suit in a video
and, surprisingly, didn't destroy his entire career in the process.

The fact that The Cure have endured where most of their
peers have perished is a credit to Smith's unique talent and obses-
sive pursuit of an ideal. For almost two decades now he has dedi-
cated himself to creating an environment that allows him to live as
master of his own universe. This unerring quest has at times
brought The Cure to the brink of destruction. And yet time after
time they have bounced back to confuse and confound all expecta-
tions of them. Along the way Smith's backcombed bouffant and
smudged lipstick have come to symbolise a refusal to compromise,
a V-sign to fashion and an antidote to manufactured pop and
clichéd rock.

Smith is an eternal teenager. One of a rare breed who still retains the idealised visions of a sussed adolescent. His ambition at fourteen was "to sit on top of a mountain and just die," and this disgust at a world built on hypocrisy has not left him. He still maintains that, of all the people he has ever met, "most of them are shit, basically." However, his recurrent sense that everything—even The Cure — is ultimately futile, has been offset by the two abiding passions in his life. Even before The Cure became Smith's raison d'être it was Mary Poole, whom he met in a drama class at school, who first showed him the possibilities that life could offer. According-ing to Smith, it is Mary's capacity to be utterly abandoned — a qual-ity that makes him both envious and jealous — that makes her a perfect balance to his own brooding and sometimes self-destructive nature.

Although early on The Cure were inevitably compared to their new wave contemporaries — The Buzzcocks, Wire, Talking Heads, and the like — Smith has always shown scant regard for his fellow musicians. His only documented obsession with a group remains The Sensational Alex Harvey Band: "He inspired two years of my life. Without him I'd have been into Supertramp, those sort of horrible groups... He was the only person who made me think, it must be fucking brilliant to be Alex Harvey. It was like believing in a myth that was presented to you on stage."

Smith had been playing the guitar since the age of seven and formed various bands while still at school. The early efforts of Malice, and later The Easy Cure, were spirited enough, but suffered from the moribund musical climate of the time which offered little direction for aspiring bands. However, as Smith approached school-leaving age, punk began to scrawl its signature across the nation's youth. Suddenly, being in a band meant more than an excuse to skip religious education classes. For Smith, already dreading the prospect of work or further education, punk was the catalyst for him to focus full-time on his passion for music.

Once he'd found the confidence to reject the path to university and a conventional lifestyle, Smith put all his energy into transforming The Easy Cure into a band he could really believe in. They had already won and lost a record contract and built up something of a local live following. Smith had quickly emerged as the leader, persuading the band to shorten their name to The Cure, and, crucially, to dispense with the 'not very punk' guitar heroics of one Porl Thompson. By the time a Polydor A&R man looking to set up his own label chanced upon their demo tape, The Cure were increasingly working from Smith's blueprint for a starker, more minimalist sound.

In December 1978 Chris Parry's new Fiction label released *Killing An Arab*, via an independent, Small Wonder. It was a peculiar little package. The sleeve featured a reversed-out photo of an old man's face; a grotesque and arresting image. The record itself was a stripped-down Moorish-flavoured guitar pattern providing background for Smith's Albert Camus-inspired paean to the trials of existence. From its opening line, *Standing on a beach with a gun in my hand*, delivered in a disinterested sneer, the song perfectly encapsulated the sense of existential vacuum left by the implosion of punk.

But if *Killing An Arab* exemplified the post-punk sound, it also contained the seeds of a new progression. At a time when many bands were struggling in vain to recapture punk's sense of urgency, the school-friend trio of Robert Smith, Laurence Tolhurst and Michael Dempsey felt too removed from London's cultural epicentre to concern themselves with jumping on any New Wave bandwagon.

For Smith especially, punk was a purely private revolution. Isolated in the satellite suburb of Crawley, his experience of punk had been listening to John Peel's late night show on *Radio 1*. It was here in the sanctuary of his bedroom that he embraced the sonic aftershock of bands like The Buzzcocks and The Clash. However, he had no intention of merely emulating what he heard; he already had ideas of his own, and the evidence pouring from his radio was that you really could 'do it yourself'. If punk had degenerated into a plastic passion, it had at least shaken the foundations of rock's hegemony. As Smith later commented: "The liberation of punk, for us, was the sense that you didn't have to be orthodox... a sense of total release."

The Cure's first album, *Three Imaginary Boys*, was released on Fiction in May 1979. Smith took an instant dislike to the record, deriding it as little more than a compilation of Easy Cure live favourites, and thus not reflecting the new direction in which he was taking the band. He was also deeply unhappy with the album's visual presentation, over which The Cure had been denied any control. The decision to feature a fridge, a Hoover and a standard lamp in place of the customary moody group shot — and to use pictures instead of song titles — was just the kind of record company interference that Smith didn't want.

There was no doubt that Fiction boss Chris Parry shared Smith's belief in The Cure, but he also had a lot riding on their success. Parry, whose previous signings included The Jam and Siouxsie And The Banshees, had set up Fiction specifically to sign The Cure. He remained impressed by their intelligence and self-confidence, but exasperated by their stubborn refusal to allow him any say in their development. The Cure were still bound together by an 'us against the world' mentality learnt from school, and Parry's demands that they sharpen up their image and upgrade their instruments met with dumb insolence.

By imposing his concept for *Three Imaginary Boys*, Parry unwittingly gave Smith the excuse he needed to insist upon absolute control of The Cure. When the time came to record *17 Seconds*, the second album, Smith presented Parry with a new line-up: Laurence Tolhurst on drums, Matthieu Hartley on keyboards, and drinking buddy Simon Gallup on bass (replacing Michael Dempsey, whose frequent opposition to Smith's musical ideas had earned him an entry in that 'long as your arm' list of ex-Cure players).

Although Hartley's tenure was also to prove a short one, this line up effectively defined The Cure sound: steady drum beats, well-defined loping bass lines and guitar used to punctuate or underline. The release of *A Forest* trademarked the distinctive sound and set a musical standard that still guides The Cure today. For, if the demands of stadium gigs have led them to expand their sound, they have never abandoned the underlying musical philosophy learnt from punk that favours economy and concise expression over guitar solos and cock-rock posturing.

Smith's transition from band member to group leader is sometimes portrayed as the act of a vanity-riddled despot, but the simple answer is that his impeccable credentials made him the natural captain of The Cure's dreamboat. It was Smith who had persuaded the original Easy Cure to ditch their restrictive contract with the teen-star obsessives at Hansa, their first label. It was Smith who had masterminded the subsequent departure that left the band with copyright to their demo, and it was Smith who had negotiated for the freedom they eventually found at Fiction. The fact that The Cure's eleventh album, *Wild Mood Swings*, followed two decades, twenty million album sales and umpteen stadium-filling performances, is vindication of Smith's basic philosophy that self-expression without compromise is the only honourable route to success.

The legendary stubbornness with which he has dragged The Cure all the way from art-school curios to stadium artists extraordinaire is a unique and compelling saga.

Many an adolescent dream is built upon the ideal of stardom, and a life defined and lived on one's own terms. Few achieve that dream and those that do discover a new set of dangers and responsibilities. In retrospect it is easy to see how Smith's passion for The Cure quickly became a dangerous obsession. If being in a band was initially a way to avoid a conventional nine-to-five existence —

or as Smith has put it, "a series of alarm calls and unendurable days" — it soon became the only reason to get up in the morning.

Whether it was a case of too much too soon, or Smith's inability to conceive of a world outside his own, The Cure's second album, *17 Seconds*, was the sound of a band growing in on itself. With no heroes to emulate and a healthy disdain for the competition, Smith was discovering that Cure songs had to be wrenched from his own psyche. This brought an intensely personal depth to The Cure's music and cemented the band into an incestuous triangle which viewed outsiders with suspicion and mistrust. Even Mary was increasingly coming second to Robert's recording and touring commitments, and the pressure this put on their relationship formed the central lyrical motif to *17 Seconds*.

In what was to become typical form, the deep waters of Smith's mind infected the atmosphere of the album. *17 Seconds* serves as a poignant elegy to the passing of carefree adolescent, seen through the eyes of a twenty-year-old. A Forest pretty much summed up the album's mood — reclusive and disturbed:

The girl was never there
It's always the same
I'm running towards nothing
again and again and again…
A Forest

At the same time, it displayed all the qualities required of a record seeking to provide a viable alternative: insufferable cool, lyrical depth and stylishly understated playing. A Forest charted at No. 31, defying the critics, who derided it for being cold, and earning The Cure their debut on *Top Of The Pops*. Stardom beckoned. But the cracks in Smith's psychological armour that would turn his passion into dysphoria and drug-induced psychosis were already beginning to show.

In addition to the pressure The Cure was putting on his relationship with Mary, Smith was finding himself ill-suited to the chaotic blur of life on the road. The experience jaded his senses and blocked his ability to write. He later admitted: "I was letting myself slip in order to write songs. I wasn't fighting it, whereas, in everyday life, you'd have to control those feelings." Ironically, it was Smith's growing reputation as the next Ian Curtis-style rock casualty that earned The Cure a devoted cult following. Smith was quick to dismiss any notion that he was prepared to die for his audience, but the emotionally charged spectacle of a Cure show left little doubt in the mind of the audience that Smith was holding nothing back in his pursuit of perfection.

Throughout their career, live shows have become the touchstone of The Cure's state of health: either intimate, moving affairs, or uncomfortable exhibitions of tension and emotional imbalance. Smith summed up the problem on 1989's Disintegration Tour: "It was brilliant to do something with that intensity, but you can't stay like that." Over the years Smith has grown more able to deal with the frustration that inevitably follows the euphoria of a dazzling live performance. But at the time of *17 Seconds* he was still searching for a sign of tangible perfection amidst the turbulence of his personal life. Mary's numerous 'me or the band' ultimatums were answered with callous honesty in *Play For Today*, the lyric *It's not a case of doing what's right, it's just the way I feel that matters* contrasting sharply with the grown up sentiments of *Lovesong* from *Disintegration*: *Whatever words I say, I will always love you.*

Smith's compulsion to express his innermost feelings in songform is what gives The Cure their lyrical edge. In an early interview he revealed: "I've always written things down, ever since I can remember. Mainly because I get really angry... I don't throw tantrums or anything like that... I go off somewhere, rather than smash the room. I write things down; it's a release."

This intensity with which Smith has carved out a place for The

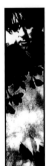

Cure in pop/rock mythology has been tempered only slightly as he matures and changes. His twin passions for Mary and the band have to some extent disentangled, allowing him to pursue an ordinary existence away from the limelight. However, he has retained the ability to draw upon the raw substance of his emotions to write and perform. The need to release the rush of pent-up feelings has kept The Cure alive.

Smith's continual pronouncements, usually after a gruelling world tour, that The Cure have reached the end of the road are inevitably followed by their return to the fray. It's just his way of keeping the band and their audience on their toes. His confession that, "if I didn't feel The Cure could fall apart at any minute it would be completely worthless," reveals the essential fragility at the band's core, a state initially imposed by Smith's chaotic self, but one that he has fostered as a ward against The Cure ever degenerating into a lumbering stadium dinosaur. Even in the midst of a live performance, the fifteen-year-old inside Robert Smith will be watching from the packed auditorium, asking the eternal question: "Is this a band I would want to be in?"

faith

Heaven give me a sign, waiting for the sun to shine.
The Baby Screams

For an avowed atheist, Robert Smith has applied himself to The Cure's cause with the faith of a Knight Templar engaged in a religious crusade. He has often referred to the early years of The Cure as being "like waging a war". If this sentiment reflects the attitude of a group formed in reaction to the mediocrity that surrounded them, it also more deeply reflects the rejection of his Catholic upbringing, that being in the Cure symbolised for Smith.

    Smith's ardent belief in the individual was forged in an atmosphere of religious indoctrination, giving it a sharper focus than most teenage rebellions. Notre Dame Middle School, where he first met Lol Tolhurst and Michael Dempsey, was at the time experimenting with a progressive, freethinking approach to education. Its emphasis on artistic expression was, ironically, the perfect environment for the various members of the proto-Cure to develop their talents. But Smith was always a natural anarchist. Notre Dame's attempts to soften the age-old religious message — namely, that toil and suffering are made palatable by the promise of an afterlife — failed to impress him. For Smith, the school's teaching methods were simply evidence of the hypocrisy that, he believed, characterised the adult world.

The fact that his early experiments in music were suffused with religious imagery was initially a con to exempt him from classes. However, as the euphoria of The Cure's early successes wore off, Smith found his Catholic upbringing returning to haunt him. *17 Seconds* had successfully conveyed an atmosphere of existential mystique informed more by the writings of Kafka and Camus than any religious text. But it was becoming clear that the tensions emerging within the band mirrored a deeper, internal conflict raging in the Smith psyche. The attractive promise of religious faith that he'd rejected outright seems to have found an affinity with Smith's own search for a meaning to his existence.

The doubt and uncertainty that had begun to afflict Smith during *17 Seconds* was compounded by two devastating events — the death of his grandmother, and Lol's mother becoming terminally ill. With The Cure about to record their third album, Smith's lack of any belief in life or existence after death became the central theme to his song writing. *Faith*, released in April 1981, was an album seeking to explore the concept of faith on different levels, and from different standpoints. Where *17 Seconds* had been a personal soundtrack to lost innocence and the ravages of time, *Faith* took those doubts and cast them into a wider sphere.

Seeking inspiration for the album, Smith had taken to visiting churches, watching the congregation in order to glean some insight into what they might be feeling. If *Faith* was conceived as an artistic statement, its concerns were uncomfortably close to home. Smith was once again experiencing the depression and sense of futility that he had felt aged fourteen. His song writing had become a catharsis, an attempt to rid himself of the last vestiges of his religion, which he felt were threatening his confidence in The Cure as his chosen lifestyle. But the more he stripped away the protective layers of his upbringing, the more he discovered only emptiness beneath. *Faith* was conceived as a positive affirmation of the spirit, pitched against the blind devotion of religious belief. However, Smith's emotional instability at the time turned it into a record of utter negation.

This unending quest to replace the vacuum left by Smith's rejection of religious faith is one of the prime reasons for The Cure's longevity. It is a theme that emerges on every successive Cure album. Smith confessed to *Q* magazine in 1987: "I feel dreadfully lonely sometimes. It's the worst feeling in the world and it's partly because I have no faith. I no longer believe in my own soul." Going on to talk about the haunting *If Only Tonight We Could Sleep*, from that year's *Kiss Me, Kiss Me, Kiss Me* album, he revealed: "In that song I'm harking back, wishing I could still believe in my guardian angel; but I know I'm just wanting something that's gone forever."

The very real and tragic events that had occurred in the lives of Robert and Lol cast a grim shadow over the *Faith* sessions. Mortality and the concept of a hereafter were no longer abstract concepts to be conjured with in the pursuit of a good record. Driven closer together by grief, The Cure retreated into the studio, fully absorbing themselves in the ceremonial ambience of those sessions.

Smith's wish was that *Faith* should be a positive record to counter the angst of *17 Seconds*. It was a wish not granted. *Faith* was a desperate and unanswered cry into the void. Songs like *The*

Holy Hour and *All Cats Are Grey*, whilst majestic and deeply reso-
nant, were uncomfortably sad and bleak. Smith's fascination with
Indian Mantras and Benedictine chants gave the music a repetitive,
hypnotic quality, adding weight to the perception in some quarters
that *Faith* was a semi-religious album. Although the opposite was
the case, the spellbound aura and macabre elegance of *Faith* alienated all those who'd viewed The Cure as saviours of the New Wave.
At the same time, it crystallized their remaining fans into a hard-
core of devoted Smith worshippers. The single Primary — one of
only two upbeat tracks — echoed the feelings of *17 Seconds*: regret at
the passing of time, the closing down of emotional honesty and the
breakdown of personal relationships that inevitably follows.

For the *NME*, who'd invested heavily in punk, The Cure were
a lost cause. It now saw them as doom-laden pariahs relentlessly
pursuing an idealised and highly unfashionable middle-class artistic
vision. *Faith* was summarily dismissed as "grammar school angst",
but for dispirited teenagers too young for the materialist aspirations
of the Thatcher years, The Cure's music provided a soundtrack to
their self-conscious despair. A whole subculture was forming
around the vortex of Smith's soul.

The Picture Tour promoting *Faith* was perhaps the greatest test
The Cure ever faced. Smith would often leave the stage crying after
pouring out his deepest fears and doubts to half-filled halls. He
commented: "We sort of wore it everywhere we went, it was like
sack cloth and ashes." The Cure even took to playing in a circus tent
to try and lift the mood, but to no avail. Audiences were becoming
increasingly hostile. Internationally, The Cure's reputation hinged
on the poppier sounds of *Three Imaginary Boys*. The low-key dynam-
ics of *The Holy Hour* and *All Cats Are Grey* — which opened their
set — were greeted with anger and disbelief. In particular, the Aus-
tralian and Canadian legs of the tour were fraught with tension. The
band often endured being jeered and pelted with cans. Robert and
Simon took to jumping into the audience to 'sort out' the culprits.

Worse was to come. Halfway through the tour Lol was told his mother had died just before a show. The band went on stage and played *Faith*'s eponymous title track. Arguably the most moving song Smith has ever written, *Faith* has become a stunning climax to The Cure's more intense live shows.

It is typical of The Cure's almost perversely unpredictable nature that, in the midst of the chaos and emotional upset that surrounded the Picture Tour, they found time to make one of their most potent singles to date. *Charlotte Sometimes* has been hailed by Cure fans as 'one of those moments', a gem among Cure songs. It has all the magic ingredients that recur from time to time across the impressive catalogue: dissonant, but with a pop heart; accessible, but aching with secret meaning; musically impenetrable, yet eminently hummable. At the time, though, it's confused brilliance was completely overshadowed by the absurd pop video that accompanied it. Director Mike Mansfield's unintentionally hilarious shoot, featuring a psychiatric hospital, a model with no talent for acting and a rather embarrassed looking Cure, was an unmitigated disaster that would haunt the band for the rest of their days. *Charlotte Sometimes* barely scraped into the Top 50, reinforcing the prevailing view of the music press that *Faith* would be The Cure's swan-song.

At Lol's insistence, the Picture Tour resumed, but by the time it reached America The Cure were a band running on empty. The death of Lol's mother and the continued hostility of audiences towards the *Faith* material were exacting a heavy toll on all of them. Only the siege mentality of the group and an increasing reliance on alcohol and drugs kept them together. No one wanted to admit defeat and so the tour staggered on. Following their second gig at the New York Ritz, Robert and Simon took an accidental overdose of Quaaludes. They were extremely lucky to survive, but the side effects — paranoia and hallucinations — lasted for days and turned their West Coast gigs into a deranged blur. Smith later revealed to Steve Sutherland: "I kept imagining people were threatening me and I was still feeling weird when we arrived in Auckland, New Zealand! It was from the hotel in Auckland that I phoned up The Banshees. I called Severin — they were on tour in Scotland at the time — and I played him *Charlotte Sometimes* down the phone. I was really proud of it. But during the phone call I fell asleep... the phone bill was $480. The next morning I was so exhausted I couldn't understand how or why I was there."

For a less committed group of individuals this would have been the end. Relations between the band were at breaking point. Mary was once again putting pressure on Smith to leave the band for the sake of their relationship and for his own mental health. Chris Parry was beginning to wonder what he'd ever seen in The Cure. Far from being the saviours of the post-punk scene, they seemed hellbent on destroying themselves and possibly taking Fiction down with them. All eyes were focused on Smith. The Cure were his baby and it was his blueprint that everyone had been following. What would he do next?

Smith reacted by shutting himself off from friends and family and spending more time with the Banshees, in particular Steve Severin. He was by now something of a minor star in his own right and, with The Cure's career at an impasse, he joined the Banshees on tour. Relieved from the pressure of making The Cure successful — for the time being at least — Smith was able to return to his former role as a hired guitar hand for The Banshees. This did little to repair his relationship with Simon. As Smith's main confidant, Simon was understandably jealous that Robert had chosen to abandon The Cure in favour of a jet-set lifestyle with Severin and Sioux.

Smith's selfishness and occasional callousness towards those around him has been the saving grace of The Cure. The overconfidence caused by early success, the steadfast refusal to compromise or heed advice, all ultimately gained The Cure the respect they needed to pursue Smith's single-minded vision of what a band should be. The prime reason they survived the wilderness that followed *Faith* was Smith's belief in The Cure as reflection of his life, rather than just an aspect of his personality. This has inevitably meant that the vitality of The Cure is closely linked to Smith's own. Their history is one of artistic peaks and troughs that tend to mirror Smith's moods. They are bound up in a never ending cycle of struggling to achieve perfection, then being dissatisfied with the results and having to start again. *Perfect moments wait*, Smith sang on *Faith*, and he would have to wait eight years for his second attempt to capture fully the concept he was striving for on *Disintegration*, released in May 1989. In particular, *The Same Deep Water As You* and *Disintegration* retread *Faith*'s unrequited themes, but they are cathedrals of sound by comparison.

It is ironic that Smith's quest for self in the absence of God has resulted in his own virtual deification. There is a mystique that surrounds The Cure that marks them out from the predictable mainstream. It inspires utter devotion from their regenerative and perpetually young audience, who appear to identify with Smith's refusal to 'grow up' or accept compromise. And then there are the songs; highly evocative psychological landscapes of meaning that resonate with a common pool of human experience. Critics have often complained that Smith's lyrics are little more than meaningless word associations, but in attempting to transcend the limits of language, Smith has hit upon the essence of pure pop communication — that inexpressible burst of transcendence that fires the imagination, yet defies explanation.

Smith has undoubtedly made mistakes along the way. However, there is nothing in The Cure's history that he would change. He has succeeded in purely personal terms through a mixture of belief in himself and contempt for any accepted way of doing things. At the start of The Cure's career, the employment service threatened to stop Smith's benefits unless he took a job they'd found for him. He retorted that they should give it to someone who wanted a job. This is the essence of Smith's attitude, and one that

has served The Cure well. He refuses to accept any standards save his own and anyone failing to meet his requirements is simply erased from his world view. His one indulgence was to allow Lol Tolhurst to remain within the band long after he had ceased to contribute anything of value. However, following Lol's unsuccessful legal action against Smith in 1994 over money matters, he too is gradually being erased from The Cure's history. Despite his close association with Smith throughout The Cure's turbulent existence, Smith now belittles his role, claiming he provided little more than company.

Smith's dismissive attitude towards anyone not sharing his vision of how The Cure should develop is sometimes seen as a sign of rampant egomania. He has always maintained that The Cure is more than just him and whoever else happens to be around. At times, though, it has been hard to discern any sort of democracy at work. Smith knows that he *is* The Cure and if necessary can resort to tyranny to achieve his aims. He has always been aware that The Cure's music might be more a form of personal therapy than a desire to say anything profound about the world. In an interview with Paul Morely in 1980, he revealed: "I've got faith in what I'm doing from a personal point of view but as to whether I go down in history, I'm very doubtful about that, so I don't let it worry me. If I let that worry me I'd crack up before I'm going to anyway."

After *Faith*, it looked as if Smith had already reached his predicted breakdown. A kind of schizophrenic madness reigned in his messed up mind, wrecking his personal relationships and pushing The Cure's music to new extremes. The next eighteen months were to prove a roller-coaster ride through hell, producing *Pornography*'s anguished cacophony as well as some of the most deranged lunatic synth-pop ever to appear on *Top Of The Pops*. By the end of it, Smith would have rediscovered his pop sensibility and brought The Cure into a new firmament of critical acclaim and chart success.

MADNESS

Get away from me. Leave me alone. Like the pig on the stairs,
hanging in a groovy purple shirt.
Give Me It

The artistic process has always been closely associated with madness. Delving deep into the self is a potentially dangerous activity and as the Cure prepared to record their fourth album, *Pornography*, Smith's inward obsessions were pushing him to the very edge of psychosis.

Smith describes the decision to make *Pornography* as the key action of his life: "I had two choices at the time, which were either giving up completely, or making a record and getting it out of me." With Smith under immense pressure to deliver an album that would restore The Cure's fortunes, the atmosphere at RAK studios was intense. Working twenty hours a day, catching brief episodes of sleep on the floor of Fiction's offices, Simon, Lol and producer Phil Thornalley — who would later join the band — struggled to interpret Smith's ideas. Often they would simply give up and get drunk, famously building a beer can mountain while Smith soldiered on maniacally. When he did join in the party antics of the others, the inevitable drugs and alcohol hangover would leave him unable to work for days after.

Smith later admitted being unable to remember vast chunks of the *Pornography* sessions. He was spending a lot of time with Steve Severin, and wrote most of the album's lyrics during what was later described as a "chemical vacation" spent wandering around London hallucinating. In addition to the obvious part played by psyche-

delics, Smith was inspired by his excessive reading in the area of mental health: the line, *A charcoal face bites my hand*, from *A Short Term Effect*, was drawn from a book in which a patient drew people in charcoal and then had nightmares in which they came alive. Other songs were closer to home: "*Hanging Garden* came about when I was at home, listening to the noises of cats outside... it made me go strange... I wanted to go out in the garden... so I did... stark naked... stupid..."

The album that finally emerged from those crazy, distorted days was an almost impenetrable tapestry of clattering percussion, phased guitars and wailing vocals. From its opening line, *It doesn't matter if we all die*, to the closing stanza, *I must fight this sickness, find a cure*, *Pornography*, released in May 1982, provided chilling yet utterly compelling insights into Smith's obsessions of the time: psychological breakdown and moral hypocrisy.

Pornography isn't an easy record to listen to. It has an air of personal revelation about it that borders on the voyeuristic. Specific meanings are camouflaged by Smith's fragmented song writing, but there is a pervading sense of a singularly Catholic guilt, both at the corruption of the world, and at his own Jekyll and Hyde morality. In an astonishingly frank interview with *Zig Zag*'s Antonella Black, Smith revealed: "My relationship with Mary is what most people would call liberal — but not in that horrible contrived sense." Nevertheless, *Pornography*'s disgust at society's corruption is intertwined with Smith's inability to deal with the consequences of his own indiscretions. The fractured narratives of both *Siamese Twins* and *The Figurehead* convey a dread of a conjugal bed which has become haunted by the memories of secret sexual liaisons.

Too many secrets
Too many lies
Writhing with hatred
Too many secrets

Please make it good tonight
But the same image haunts me
In sequence, in despair of time
I will never be clean again
The Figurehead

For the press, *Pornography* was final proof that The Cure had burnt their brains to ash with the radiant heat of their own imaginings. "Phil Spector in Hell," was the pronouncement of the *NME*. But despite negative reviews, The Cure's growing fanbase gave *Pornography* a No. 8 chart placing, hardening Smith's conviction that the torturous path they were following was the right one.

The Fourteen Explicit Moments tour that followed made the ill-fated Picture Tour seem like a picnic by comparison. In thrall to *Pornography*'s savage imagery, the band wore lipstick around their eyes and mouths. As they sweated under the spot lights, their faces looked as though they were bleeding. It was pure theatre, but behind the make-up the aggression was all too real. Fights would regularly break out backstage and the tension between Robert and Simon was clearly visible on stage. Smith had retreated into an unpleasant world of his own, refusing to communicate. Simon was, according to Parry, a "lost soul". He already felt betrayed by Smith's friendship with Severin and now, virtually isolated from Smith, was becoming bitter and paranoid. Smith later admitted in *Ten Imaginary Years*: "People couldn't speak to me because I wanted everyone else to be as I was. You had to actually want to be part of it and people hated us, hated those concerts, even most Cure fans."

Eventually the tension that had been building throughout the tour erupted in a club after a gig in Strasbourg with a violent punch-up between Robert and Simon. The Cure effectively split, returning to England separately. It would be eighteen months before Robert and Simon saw each other again.

Pornography was a desperate cry from a band on the verge of self-annihilation, but Smith had purged his worst nightmares in public and The Cure could never be that extreme again. The band's temporary demise gave him a badly needed breathing space. To his surprise, as much as anyone else's, he found himself writing again. The result was *Lament*, recorded with Steve Severin for *Flexipop* magazine. Although achingly nostalgic, the sessions, which took place in the wilds of Wales, were relaxed and amiable, and gave an insight into how Smith's lyrical intensity could be wedded to pop.

After *Pornography*, Smith realised something important about The Cure. "The group is there to escape the oppressiveness, it's a way of screaming," he said. Sensing this change of attitude, Chris Parry persuaded Smith to write a throwaway pop single, something unlike The Cure, that would break the mould and destroy the myth of the band as humourless, angst-ridden goths. Smith set about writing the most inane, lightweight lyric he could think of and included all the worst synthesiser sounds he despised. The upshot was *Let's Go To Bed* and its B-side *Just One Kiss*. Smith immediately realised that the songs were not bad enough and argued that they should be released under the name Recur. However, he was feeling sufficiently destructive towards The Cure that, when Parry offered him a deal that would release him from his contract if *Let's Go To Bed* flopped, he capitulated.

Determined to go the whole hog with their cynical chart ploy, Parry introduced Smith to Tim Pope, a young video director whose videos for Soft Cell they both admired. Smith and Pope hit it off and formed a working relationship which would change the image of The Cure forever. In *Ten Imaginary Years* Pope recalled: "I began to push him more and more because he had never performed in a video before. That's where we started to breed and develop that eccentric little character which we now all know and love! I don't know why, I saw him as a clown — funny, but also tragic."

Apart from Pope's hilarious video which featured such insane antics as Smith's wearing finger puppets and Lol imitating Tears

For Fears' robotic dancing, *Let's Go To Bed* failed spectacularly to achieve its aim. It received virtually no airplay and made Top 50 rather than the Top 20 Parry was banking on. Smith spent most of his promotional airtime slagging it off and, to Parry's further fury, joined the Banshees full-time for their British tour. Parry threatened to sue. Smith threatened to break his legs. Rumours of a Cure split abounded once more.

Smith's relationship with Severin was one built around a love of hedonism and trash psychedelia. Between March and May 1983 they embarked upon a long-nurtured side project, The Glove, named after the murder mitten in The Beatles' *Yellow Submarine*. Smith has always cited Severin as something of a bad influence: "We were never very good for each other." The sort of crazy logic by which the pair decided that a diet of LSD and bad horror movies was the way to make a good album had Severin's stamp all over it. Smith later told *Melody Maker*: "It was an attack on the senses... We were coming out of the studio at six in the morning, watching all these really mental films, then going to sleep and having these really demented dreams and then, as soon as we woke up at four in the afternoon, we'd go straight back into the studio. It was a bit like a mental assault course by the end." The resulting LP *Blue Sunshine* was the kind of acid-dazed nonsense that was only to be expected.

Smith was now captain of two Cures; a one-man psychedelic band and the older, doomier model waiting in the wings. When The Cure were offered a slot on BBC TV's *Oxford Road Show*, Smith refused their suggestion that he perform *Let's Go To Bed* and *Just One Kiss*. To everyone's horror, he opted instead to play *The Figurehead* and *One Hundred Years* with a cobbled together band that included Brilliant's Andy Anderson on drums and Derek Thompson from SPK on bass. The experience rekindled Smith's interest in The Cure, and he was soon back in the studio working on a follow-up to *Let's Go To Bed*. If die-hard fans were heaving sighs of relief that The Cure were back on form, Smith had other plans. Recruiting electronics ace Steve Nye from Japan, he embarked on a more serious dance track which combined the gravity of *One Hundred Years* with irresistible chart chumminess.

The Walk, released in July 1983, rocketed The Cure into the Top 20 and paved the way for eventual massive success. Tim Pope was once again called upon to interpret the distorted dream images of Smith's mind. This time he excelled himself. The cross-dressing capers of Robert and Lol, along with the recurring glob of what closely resembled human sperm, got the video banned by the BBC.

The Love Cats, inspired by Disney's *The Aristocats*, completed the dream-pop trilogy and marked the Cure down as mischievous scoundrels purveying cheeky pop tunes. Smith had now achieved pop stardom, appearing in *Smash Hits* and adorning the bedroom walls of fourteen-year-old schoolgirls. He was quick to dismiss cries of 'sell out' from the by now bemused legion of fans who'd been hoping for a return to the sombre days of *A Forest*. He told *Sounds*: "It's like we're their pet band and how dare I tamper with our mysterious image. I never asked for blind devotion. I resent it, because they're trying to shrink me into a one-faceted person who's only allowed to produce one style of music."

Despite Smith's determination to turn his back on The Cure's troubled past, he was far from happy with his new-found status as teen-pop idol. In the wake of the dream-pop compilation album *Japanese Whispers*, released in December 1983, Smith's new-found public expected more of the same. They were rewarded with *The Caterpillar* in May of the following year. However, no one was prepared for *The Top* album released simultaneously. Never before, or since, has pop sounded so terrifying. Ranging from summery psychedelia to brute violence and misogyny, *The Top* suggested that reports of Smith's mental recovery had been greatly exaggerated. If the pop numbers — *Piggy In The Mirror*, *Bananafishbones*, *Birdmad Girl* — were certifiable, the protracted scream of *Give Me It* was hardly music at all, more an aggressive burst of confused loathing.

Get away from me
Leave me alone
Like the pig on the stairs
Hanging in a groovy purple shirt
Give Me It

Smith had finally lost the plot. The madness he had been courting since the early days had taken control, warped creativity dripping from every pore. Working almost alone — Lol is credited with 'other instruments' — and dividing his time between touring with the ailing Banshees and making *The Top*, he was chasing every last ounce of creative energy. For, deep down, Smith was well aware that he would eventually have to take stock of all that had happened to The Cure, and his own mental state since *Pornography*.

Tim Pope, now established as The Cure's video maestro, has come closest to understanding the bundle of contradictions that make up Smith's character. It is largely thanks to him that the latter-day image of The Cure is of a quirky, humorous band capable of outlandish cartoon capers as well as profound insights into the human condition. Without him, they might have gone down in history as morose outcasts who could never have appealed to a mass audience. In *Ten Imaginary Years*, Pope gave his verdict on Smith at the time of compiling the video singles collection *Standing On A Beach*: "He's a paradoxical character. Everything he is, he isn't. He's very pretentious, but he isn't. He's always black, yet he's white, and The Cure are one of the stupidest bands you could ever work with, yet they're the brightest, the most intelligent. They're the noisiest but they can be the quietest — that's what I love about them. Robert says he's like a child but he isn't, he's too intelligent. Since *Head On The Door*, he's changed."

This last comment pinpoints the moment when Smith successfully synthesised his need to oust his inner demons through song with his latent pop sensibility. Songs like *In Between Days* and *Close*

To Me, while still spine-tinglingly demented, were imbued with a riotous pop-tinged celebration of the absurd. The eminently more loveable tragic clown image of Smith captured in Pope's videos allowed The Cure to appeal to a wider audience whilst effectively healing the rift with the older fans alienated by the wilful destruction of *Let's Go To Bed*. The Cure had finally achieved Smith's ambition to be a commercially successful alternative to the drab MOR of Elton John and Phil Collins.

With the arrival of fame, Smith has been subjected to unwelcome media attention. An intensely private person, he has reacted by making up stories rather than revealing any true details of his personal life. He once told *The Daily Mirror* that his parents took acid and that Mary was a stripping nurse. Many gullible editors reprinted his claim that he had taken a live lamb on tour. Various reasons were given. In one version, he found it in his hotel room. In another, a fan gave it to him and it was now living on his brother's farm in Wales.

Smith is an unlikely pop star. Despite the helpless 'cuddle me' image he portrays on screen, he is clearly a shrewd businessman and skilled manipulator of The Cure's fortunes. At times he seems to court enigma and yet his private persona is almost disappointingly normal. It's as if he has mastered the art of separating his scatological Cure persona from the decent chap who likes a pint and a game of football. His comment at the time of *The Head On The Door* that, "I would be dead if I'd lived through everything I write about," is typical of his tendency to draw a smokescreen over his jealously guarded privacy.

More likely, if he *hadn't* sung about all those things, he'd be dead. The paradox is that The Cure can be an escape route, but also a trap; a remedy, but also the cause of the sickness. As Smith has admitted: "That's part of the make-up of someone who's in the group. You don't stop doing something just because you know it's going to do you harm. That would be very boring."

DESIRE

The blindness of happiness, of falling down laughing, and I really believed that this time was forever.

Last Dance

Images of drowning, suffocation and falling abound in the visual landscape of Cure songs. At times they symbolise Smith's compulsion to give in to what he calls *"the devil futility"*; at others, his need to be swept away by intense peaks of emotion. The idea of 'surrender' that these images evoke is central to Smith's desire to be released from his perpetual struggle to find meaning in the routine humdrum of life. Often the experience to which Smith wishes to surrender is an idealised notion of romantic love. Love, after all, has the capacity to take people outside the prison of their own thoughts and return them to that state of childish wonderment that Smith has fought to preserve in himself.

However, much as Smith idealises the power of love, it sits awkwardly with his existential fear of human closeness. He professes to feeling uneasy about being comfortable and, moreover, to a desire to drive away those who love him. Love, for Smith, implies giving up his unique qualities as a human being and submerging them in a larger entity. In an interview with *Lime Lizard* he described love as "drowning into another person... you exhale your last breath, you take in water — there's no choice, so the next breath you take is death."

This almost gothic vision of love as sensory overload has become welded to the sense of fatalism that underpins Smith's view of romantic entanglements. With the exception of *Lovesong*, which he reputedly wrote for Mary as a wedding present, almost all the tracks on *Disintegration* are elegies to love's dying flame. Songs like *The Same Deep Water As You* or *Plainsong*, whilst attaining majestic heights of adoration, are infused with melancholia at the inevitability that passion must fade. Even The Cure's poppier love songs — *Just Like Heaven* or *High* from 1992's *Wish* album — end with Smith losing the object of his desire.

Paradoxically, it is Smith's sense of time and human selfishness eventually laying waste to love that gives The Cure's love songs much of their impact. He has become a master of narrating passion to its peak of intensity, then killing it off, as if death is the only way to preserve the moment forever. Or, as he rather prosaically puts it to *Lime Lizard*'s Britt Collins: "I've been knocked down by a bus... I love you."

This freezing of heartfelt moments at the point of death is a theme that has grown stronger since Smith put his nursery nightmares to bed with *The Head On The Door*. In *If Only Tonight We Could Sleep*, from The Cure's *Kiss Me, Kiss Me, Kiss Me* album, Smith implores his guardian angel to release him and his lover from their mortal constraints, thus allowing them to sleep forever.

If only tonight we could sleep
In a bed made of flowers
If only tonight we could fall
In a deathless spell

If only tonight we could slide
Into deep black water
And breathe
If Only Tonight We Could Sleep

But there is another side to Smith's preoccupation with love. If only as a concept, love fits neatly into his belief that you can live life on your own terms, shunning the conventions and moral corruption of the world. Though this attitude stems from his ardent individualism, it is surely tainted by a Catholic fear of the flesh. Smith is constantly striving to reach heaven's gate, but can never quite escape the pull of his own desire for visceral thrills. And for all their transcendental power, The Cure are at their most compelling when they descend into the lusty realm of us mortals, brought low by Smith's guilty fascination with his own sexual desires.

Tonight I'm screaming like an animal
Tonight, oh, I'm getting so low
And all I want is to be with you again
And all I want is to hold you like a dog
All I Want

Waiting for The Cure to appear on stage during the 1987 Kissing Tour, the Wembley Arena audience were treated to a video screen close-up of a pair of lips so vast they seemed in danger of swallowing the arena whole. The image, taken from the *Kiss Me* album cover, reflects Smith's mixture of repulsion and fascination for mouths. In the *Lime Lizard* interview Smith explained: "There's a taste or a smell, a degree of intimacy to do with mouths... when you're watching what other people do with their mouths, it's quite horrible, really." The spectacle of the lips was doubly disturbing given the wah-wah howl of *The Kiss* with its venom-drenched lyric which opened the shows.

Kiss me, kiss me, kiss me
Your tongue is like poison
So swollen it fills up my mouth
Love me, love me, love me
You nail me to the floor
And push my guts all inside out
The Kiss

Smith went on to reveal: "I find the human body generally repulsive and always feel hampered by being inside my body. Not because I find it particularly horrible, but just because it doesn't do enough." Elsewhere on *Kiss Me* Smith's confused mixture of hatred and lust for flesh reaches extremes reminiscent of *Pornography*:

It tortures me to move my hands
To try to move at all
And pulled
My skin so tight it screams
And screams and screams
And screams for more
Torture

In a medium where sex is usually portrayed in rock-'n'-roll clichés, Smith exposes the dark underbelly of carnal intimacy. Few songwriters could deliver the line, *All I want is to hold you like a dog*, without falling about laughing, or the virginal paranoia of *Close To Me* without cringing with embarrassment. Smith's triumph is that he never spares himself. His most private dilemmas and deepest urges are thrown into the songs to be voraciously consumed by his audience, many of whom feel they know Smith as well as his closest friends. They don't, of course. Like any performer, the feelings Smith articulates through The Cure are amplified, stylised through imagery, and bear little resemblance to the real Robert Smith.

However, if Smith does to some extent live his life through the songs of The Cure, it is hardly surprising that many of his fans seek to do the same. The track *End* from *Wish*, released in April 1992, has become one of the most talked about and studied songs of Smith's career. In it, he appears to be trying to distance himself from the audience, rejecting those personae that have been projected on to him.

Please stop loving me
Please stop loving me
I am none of these things
I am none of these things
End

Smith has said of this refrain, which at the time sounded as if it might be the final song from the final album: "In one sense it's me addressing myself. It's about the persona I sometimes fall into. On another level it's addressed to people who expect me to know things and have answers... I had it in the back of my mind when I wrote the song that when it comes to performing on the tour, it would remind me I'm not reducible to what I'm doing. People are waiting for me and The Cure to stand for something. All that nearly drove me round the bend. And I don't need any encouragement."

The question of how much longer Smith can keep raging against the dying of the light — to paraphrase his favourite poet, Dylan Thomas — is obviously one that concerns him. Smith has been careful not to let The Cure degenerate into a parody of themselves. After he'd finished tidying up the live video released after the Wish tour, he was again besieged by doubts. In an interview with the *NME* in June 1995, he told Simon Williams: "It reached a point that I'd watched it so much I fucking hated us... I hated every move I made on stage, everything about it. I cut my hair off, cut down on the make-up and thought what can I do now that's really out of character? So I went to the races. I read and talked to people. I saw my niece and nephew and thought I should impose upon them the idea that I was actually their uncle rather than have them just see pictures of me. And I became anonymous. It's not that difficult. People say it's really hard when you're in the public eye to get out of it. It isn't! You just go home for a while and don't have a publicist."

It has become pointless trying to speculate how much longer Smith can hold the intensity of his vision. In the meantime we should be thankful that The Cure are still with us. Glancing back at their peers who have perished, be they punk, new wave or goth, it is utterly remarkable that The Cure haven't imploded in a similar drug-crazed, success-phased orgy of destruction.

Smith insists that The Cure isn't Robert Smith and whoever-else-happens-to-be-there. And it's true, The Cure couldn't create the atmosphere they do with anonymous session players. The 1996 line-up — with the exception of drummer Jason Cooper — was in fact drawn from the rich lineage of sometime Cure pals and players: Perry Bamonte, Roger O'Donnell and of course Simon Gallup. The membership may fluctuate, but The Cure are practically a global institution. Their colossal status means they no longer collect the critical plaudits they often deserve, but even the hardest nosed hack harbours a degree of respect for their dogged aspiration to be the best at what they do.

If it's difficult to fit The Cure into any of the 'scenes' that have emerged in the past twenty years, this is because they have never been part of any search for the zeitgeist or cutting edge. Throughout much of their career they have been accused of being too much a hermetically sealed unit, out of touch with musical developments. But then The Cure were always completely self-referential. They have never sounded like anyone except themselves — a sound and an image built up through experimentation over many years. Smith always doubted that he'd ever earn a place in pop's pantheon as a non singer, non player with little to say about important issues or world events, but amazingly he has. The Cure occupy a whole musical and artistic genre unlike (with the possible exception of REM) any other world-class group.

While new bands continue to plunder pop's past for inspiration, none dare copy the atonal singing or chiming flange chords of The Cure. They have made such signifiers their own, and for any other to adopt them would trigger unfavourable comparisons. Cynics might claim that it is precisely these signifiers that make The Cure predictable, boring even. But Smith's humour, scatological persona and almost pathological fear of 'being shit' mean that the medium of The Curesong (TM) is constantly expanding.

Not even Smith has a firm handle on what The Cure stand for any more, if indeed they 'stand' for anything. Truth has become stranger than fiction for The Cure. The irony of recording the theme tune for the block-busting *Judge Dread* movie cannot have escaped Smith's attention. This schizophrenic perception of The Cure as miserablists who also write great pop songs has come to be accepted both by Smith and by The Cure's audience. There is such an unmistakable Cure atmosphere that pervades their recent albums, that songs as diverse as the heartbreaking *From The Edge Of The Deep Green Sea* and the joyfully escapist *Doing The Unstuck* can co-exist in perfect harmony.

If anything sets The Cure apart from the musical mass it is their power to articulate the full range of human desire, from its most bestial lows to its highest spiritual summits. Lips and eyes and animal screams, angels and demons and the darkest oceans, beguile the senses and remind us of a life outside our own. There is the sense that a true appreciation of beauty recognises its fleeting existence, that one man's love is another man's poison, that our dreams of the world contain images of rapture, yet scenes of horror. The Cure make music that alters our perception and in so doing alters our world.

 END

Daniel Patton is a 28-year-old writer and journalist living in London. He began his career on independent music magazine Outlook and has contributed to a number of books and magazines, including How Does It Feel, the first book on Oasis. He has been a contributing editor for London Calling Internet and an in-house writer for the UK division of the world's largest online publishing company, America Online.

■ Sources: Lime Lizard, Britt Collins (Lime Lizard 1991) / Zig Zag, Antonella Black (Pogo Publishing 1985) / Ten Imaginary Years, Barbarian, Steve Sutherland, Robert Smith (Zomba Books/Fiction Records 1988) / Success, Corruption & Lies, Ross Clarke (Kingsfleet Publications 1992) / The Cure: Faith, Dave Bowler & Bryan Dray (Sidgwick & Jackson 1995) / NME, Simon Williams (IPC June 24, 1995) ■ Page 4: Q&A on Canada's Jam! Music forum, August 1996 by permission Jam! Music on CANOE – http://www.canoe.ca/JamMusic ■ Photograph of Daniel Patton by Vince Goodsell ■ Designed by Philip Garner ■ Typeset by Wordset, email: wordset@londonci.demon.co.uk 0171 - 727 3776 ■ Printed by The Pale Green Press (0171 538 5180) ■ First published 1997 ■ © The Dunce Directive, PO Box 3120, London NW8 7BQ ■ Internet: http://www.london-calling.co.uk/dunce.html, email: dunce@londonci.demon.co.uk ■ All rights reserved. No part of this publication may be reproduced, stored in a retrieval system or transmitted in any way or by any means without the prior written permission of the copyright holder. ■ ISBN 0 9522068 1 1 ■ Strange as angels ■